Secrets In Every Word

Secrets In Every Word

Ultimate Tennis Success
for
Any Level of Player

Juan Farrow

Copyright © 2009 by Juan Farrow.

ISBN: Hardcover   978-1-4363-8893-1
       Softcover   978-1-4363-8892-4

All rights reserved. No part of this book may be reproduced or transmitted in any form or by any means, electronic or mechanical, including photocopying, recording, or by any information storage and retrieval system, without permission in writing from the copyright owner.

This book was printed in the United States of America.

To order additional copies of this book, contact:
Xlibris Corporation
1-888-795-4274
www.Xlibris.com
Orders@Xlibris.com
37259

Contents

Chapter 1: Winning in the beginning 11

Chapter 2: Utilizing your time properly............................. 14

Chapter 3: Winning mentally... 18

Chapter 4: Ultimate goal in tennis..................................... 21

Chapter 5: The Advantage and disadvantage of the serve........ 24

Chapter 6 The receivers' mental guide against strong serve...... 27

Chapter 7: Unnecessary confusion..................................... 30

Chapter 8: Keep Coming.. 33

Chapter 9: The pros and cons of a good topspin forehand...... 37

Chapter 10: Winning strategies... 42

Chapter 11: Footwork... 46

Chapter 12: Serving and volleying....................................... 51

Chapter 13: Strokes and footwork technique 55

    a. Topspin forehand...55
    b. One hand topspin backhand.............................56
    c. Flat inside out forehand.....................................58
    d. Flat backhand 59
    e. Forehand volley...59
    f. Backhand volley...61
    g. Backhand and forehand half volley..................62
    h. Overheads..63
    i. Topspin forehand and backhand lob................64

Chapter 14   Serve techniques 67

    a. First serve 67
    b. Second serve 70

Chapter 15   Balance and placement... 72

    a. Two handed topspin backhand..........................73
    b. One handed slice backhand...............................74

I dedicate this book to my Lord and savior Jesus Christ. I give him all thanks praise and glory, for without him I am nothing. He brought Dr. Robert Walter Johnson into my life at age four. The lord let me know through Dr. Johnson that tennis would be a major part of my life for all of my life. Dr. Johnson gave me my start. He was the foundation of everything I know. The magnitude of his contribution, not only in my tennis life, but my entire life is immeasurable. Without him, my life would be a great loss.

—Juan Farrow

Forward

Juan Farrow is the best player and coach that I've had the honor of working with, on and off the court.

The concepts, tactics, and strategies be it tactically or mentally is spot on. Jay as I call him, with his compassion and generosity, has not only made a tremendous impact on my game and teaching style, but my life as well.

I trust and believe by reading his words, secrets will be revealed to take your game to new heights.

—Parrish Preston

Many are called but few are chosen... tennis being the vehicle for us to meet. It has been a "good ride" and we are yet surfing... I'm so thankful that Lord saw fit for our paths to cross... now, then, and of course... eternally...

— your friend
Parrish Preston

Chapter One

Winning in the beginning

It is very important to start well when you are playing a match. Everyone has their share of highs and lows during a match. If you start well when the low period comes you won't have to play catch up, because you will probably be up in the match.

The main key in starting well is minimizing your unforced errors. If you are able to keep your unforced errors down to about one per game for the first three games, then your chance of being ahead in the match when your low period comes is around ninety per cent.

There are unforced errors and there are bad unforced errors. Unforced errors are usually made because you didn't give yourself enough room for error. The results are usually missing in the top of the net, or barely missing the line. Bad unforced errors are usually caused by a total malfunction in the technical or the mental department, which usually results in missing in the middle or the bottom part of the net, a foot and a half or more over the base line or wide.

For the first three games it is important to hit everything at half speed and at least two feet over the net. It is also important to hit everything at least a foot inside the baseline and sidelines. This will allow you to gain confidence a lot faster. Every player experiences being nervous, especially in the first few games of the match. With this method you should lose your nervous feeling by the end of the third game mainly because you should be making very few unforced errors.

Being aware of your opponent during the warm up is another important factor in having a good start. In most tournaments or competitions, players are usually given five minutes for warm up. At least two and a half minutes of that warm-up time should be spent getting your timing. The remaining time should be spent getting a feel for your opponent's likes and dislikes. If you are averaging one unforced error per game in the first three games and you find yourself down a service break or three zero, don't panic, quickly ask yourself a series of questions, and be honest with your answers. This shouldn't take you no more than forty five seconds. The remaining fifteen seconds should be spent solving the problem. Remember: Once you ask yourself a question, your mind will automatically give you an honest answer. Accept the answer and move on to the next question.

Below are some questions you should ask yourself if you are making very few unforced errors and find yourself losing the match:

1. If I keep playing the same, can my opponents play sustain?
2. Do I need to increase the speed on my shots?
3. Am I hitting with too much power?
4. Am I mixing up the pace and spins on my shots?

Secrets In Every Word

5. What are my opponent's strengths and weaknesses?
6. What am I doing well?
7. Where am I missing?

You may not be aware of this, but these questions have already been thought of by you whether consciously or subconsciously-during the first three games. So the proper question automatically will come with the honest answer. Remember it is very important that split-second questions and answers are used. This way you will not spend too much time on one thought.

Chapter Two

Utilizing your time properly

When you are serving, at least ten of the 20 seconds you have between points should be spent on preparing your serve for the next point. Say approximately four words as quickly as possible. Your mind will automatically associate the word in the proper category without you having to think anymore about it. You should say no more than four words in the technical and mental categories. The words may be subject to change, depending on how good or bad your opponent is returning your serve.

For example: If you serving in the deuce court, prior to serving you should say to yourself quickly a series of words: Here are some technical words: Back straight, head up, shoulders up, stand tall and use the legs. Here are some mental words: slice flat, topspin, wide, down the middle, into the body, fast, medium, specific spot. Try to refrain from speaking to yourself in sentences, mainly because you will usually spend too much time on one thought.

Secrets In Every Word

The remaining five seconds of your service preparation time should be spent on preparing yourself for the return from your opponent. You should have a good idea where your opponent will go by the type of serve you hit. The type of serve you hit, along with your attitude when you hit it, plays a major part in your being on the offense or defense after your opponents returns the ball.

If you are receiving a serve, you should keep your eyes on the ball that your opponent is serving until the point is over. While your opponent is preparing to serve, you should take approximately fifteen seconds to think about four technical or mental words. The words are subject to change depending on how well or poorly you are returning or how well your opponent is serving. Also, the word or words you use may change if your opponent is serving a first or second serve.

For Example: You must hit the ball out in front, some words to use would be, Hit in front of left hand, or hit in front of right foot. Some mental words could be: Half volley return, hit it on the rise, move diagonally. Remember, just say the word or words you need as quickly as possible. Your mind will automatically place them with the proper thought.

The minute and a half you have when changing sides is very important to your performance once play continues. During the changeover, immediately relax and visualize yourself hitting volleys groundstroke's serves and return of serves and overheads.

When you are in a baseline rally, it is very important to be aware of your opponent's court positioning on the baseline. If your opponent is a foot or so behind the baseline, your technical and mental words would be different than if your opponent is four feet or so behind the base line. These are technical and mental words and statements that you should use if your opponent is on top of the base line or a few inches inside or behind it: Attack ball, firm/short backswing, hit deep to corner, back opponent up, make half volley.

If your opponent is too close to the baseline they are vulnerable because they are not ready in a way that would allow them to play good defense. For example: If you drive the ball using seventy-five percent power a foot and a half inside the baseline and singles sideline, then hit your next shot to the opposite sideline with the same power your opponent should be on defense.

These are some technical and mental words and statements that you should use if your opponent is four feet or more behind the base line: Run opponent in alley, slice the ball low and short, topspin hit to angles, stay down keep head still. If your opponent is four feet or more behind the baseline two new strategies should also come to mind. The first is to topspin your groundstroke's, running your opponent into the alley. When you apply this strategy remember it will be most effective if you hit short angles. This will keep your opponent on the defense; even if they guess right they will still be in the alley.

Another effective strategy if your opponent is four feet or more behind the baseline: hit a ball that will bring your opponent across the baseline a foot and a half or so. Then hit a ball deep enough to back them up at least four feet or more behind the base line. This strategy will be most effective if the ball you hit to bring them across the baseline is hit low with under-spin, or side-spin, and the ball you hit to back your opponent up is hit with maximum topspin, clearing the net six feet or so.

Your opponent should be on the defense because the low slice you hit to bring them across the baseline puts them in an uncomfortable position if they decide to come to the net because they are too deep in the court to get a good net position which will allow you to have more time to hit your passing shot. If they decide to go behind the baseline four feet or so they are on defense because the topspin forehand or backhand you hit with angle and power, along with six feet or so net clearance, will force them to hit off their back foot.

Chapter Three

Winning Mentally

Do not send your opponents any signs that will let them know that your physical or mental state is negative. When your opponent looks at you anytime during the match, they should feel uneasy no matter if they are winning, losing, or the match is even. The uneasy feeling should happen within them because of the positive attitude they see when they look at you before or after the points. Even if you are losing badly, when your opponent looks at you they should see a player who is thinking and trying to figure out how they can turn the match around. Your opponent should feel from looking at you, that they cannot let up at all.

They should feel unsure even if they are winning. It's like the Ali Frazier boxing matches. Ali was scoring points by out boxing Frazier, but with Frazier positive mental attitude, Ali knew that he could not afford to make a mistake, because Frazier would knock him out.

Many players and coaches are not aware of just how important the visual messages you give your opponents really are. Be aware of what goes through your mind when you look at your opponent before during and after points. Think about what your opponent must be thinking when they look at you before during or after a point. Be aware of what your opponent is saying and how it makes you feel. Think about what you are saying and how your opponent must feel if they hear what you have said.

Whether you know it or not you mind is aware of what your eyes are seeing. Even though you are concentrating on things pertaining to something totally different, your mind is receiving information from what you see. Therefore, split-second thinking is of the ultimate importance when you are thinking about something that you see, even though you are concentrating on something else, for example: you have made up your mind where you are going to serve and just before you are going to serve and just before you toss the ball you see your opponent leaning ever so slightly in the direction you are going to serve. Your eyes have given you vital information. Every player should have their game plan and not worry about what their opponent is doing. If you are able to incorporate knowing what's important about things you see and hear from your opponent as well as yourself you should have overwhelming confidence.

Here are ten things that you should know that will give you immediate confidence.

1. If your opponent has a one-handed backhand look to see what grip they are holding before you serve. If they are holding a slice backhand grip then you should know that if you serve the ball with medium

power and, somewhat deep, they will slice the return back ninety percent of the time. If your opponent has a topspin backhand grip and you serve the ball with medium pace making them stretch wide them they will slice the return and it will not be effective.

2. If your opponent has a two-handed backhand and you can make them take one giant step with a medium pace serve to their backhand the return usually will not be effective.
3. Know that a person with a two-hand backhand returns better from that side than the forehand.
4. If your opponent has a one-handed backhand and you hit a kick serve above their shoulder, their return usually will not be effective.
5. If you have an opponent that is saying negative things, smashing balls into the fence, or throwing rackets this should give you confidence.
6. If you opponent has changed their style of play to do what they don't really like to do.
7. Your opponent is slicing their backhand 90 percent of the time.
8. Your opponent if making bad errors periodically off super routine balls.
9. If your opponent has trouble hitting topspin, then they will have trouble hitting flat crosscourt. Do not worry about them getting you into the alley.
10. If your opponent has a two handed back hand and you make them hit a one-handed backhand on your terms.

Chapter Four

Ultimate Goal in Tennis

If you are on the baseline, your ultimate goal should be making your opponent hit you short medium high balls. This will allow you to hit an outright winner or have an easy put away, volley or overhead at the net.

If you're at the net, your ultimate goal should be making your opponent hit you a lob, or try to pass you while backing up. This in most cases will force your opponent to hit short high ball, which will allow you to hit a winning volley or over head. A very important point to keep in mind is to not hit an approach shot, volley or overhead crosscourt to your opponents forehand unless you are sure it will put your opponent in trouble or win the point out right.

Five things to remember that should help you reach your ultimate goal:

1. When you are on the baseline and your opponent's ball is hit halfway between the singles sideline and the

middle of the court, get your opponent in the alley by hitting a backhand or forehand crosscourt.
2. If you are a giant step in front of the baseline and able to make a good step into the ball, your opponent should be in trouble.
3. When you are volleying a ball that is well below the net, in most cases go deep down the line. If the ball is net level or higher, in most cases angle the ball off crosscourt.
4. If you opponent has hit a good lob and you know you are not able to put the overhead away, hit your overhead hard and deep as possible to their backhand side and come right back to the net.
5. If your opponent comes to the net, consider hitting a lob over their backhand side. When you are about to hit a passing shot, consider hitting the ball soft and low.

When you are in a baseline rally you should immediately get the feel of how important it is to have a good down the line backhand. If you and your opponent is trading crosscourt backhands whoever hits the strongest backhand down the line will, in most cases will win the point. To get a better understanding of how important it is to have a good backhand down the line think about what the majority of players are trying to accomplish during the rally. They are trying to run around their backhand to hit a strong forehand into their opponent's backhand side. In during this they make themselves vulnerable to a well hit backhand down the line. Keep in mind that even though your opponent may know that you can hit your backhand down the line, they don't feel under pressure because they feel that it's a low percentage shot. They also know that if you do not hit the ball close enough to the singles sideline you will be on the defense.

Players who are just keeping balls in play waiting for their opponent to miss have more difficulty with attaining the ultimate goal than player who is aggressive and looking to win points. If you are one of these types of players you must minimize your opponent's power by hitting low slice, or sidespin balls that skid and break into or away from his body. This will give you more breathing room because not only will they have to decrease their power, but the odds of them making errors increases. Keep in mind that a well executed slice will result in you winning the point at least fifty per cent of the time. The percentage may depend on how well your opponent handles low balls. You must know that if your serve has decent power and you are varying the spin, pace and direction you have a good chance of winning the point.

Above all, remember that when you are trying to get ahead in the point in many situations consider hitting the ball soft and low while varying the spin. This can be just as effective, if not more than hitting with power.

Chapter Five

The Advantage and Disadvantage of the Serve

There is no reason for anyone to have a first or second serve that is not a weapon. Serving is the only time in the game of tennis that you get to hit a ball without it being hit to you first. This means you have two opportunities to win the point immediately.

There are a lot of players that are known for having a strong first serve, but their are very few players who are known for having a second serve that is as strong as there first.

Their desire to keep from double faulting suffocates the confidence of knowing that they will not double fault. This mentality usually results in a defensive second serve which gives your opponent confidence every time you miss a first serve.

If you miss a first serve or a second serve it is essential that you immediately know the reason why. Keep in mind that even though you may have done a few things wrong, in most cases it's usually one specific thing that actually is the cause of the error.

The key to having an offensive second serve is attacking the ball with the same mental intensity as you do when you are hitting your hardest first serve. The difference is that you should be hitting it with slice or topspin instead of flat. Keep in mind you should be as confident in your second serve as you are in your first . . . and vice versa.

There are many players who prefer to use their first serve to start the point, rather than win it. This is a good tactic to use in the beginning of the match. Usually If a player has a higher percentage of the first serves in they will be neutral after their opponents return, because the opponent is not trying to hit a winner off their first serve. However, as the match continues, it does not take long before this tactic to become a disadvantage, especially if you are playing a high quality opponent. You may be able to get away with insufficient power only if you are varying your direction and spin. But as

you get deeper into the match you find that even with good placement on your first serve, you will feel pressure because you will be winning very few free points off your first serve due to its lack of power.

When you are serving a second serve, consider hitting it into your opponent's body. This will allow you to increase your power without the fear of double faulting. Your confidence should increase also because your opponent will have a difficult time putting you on defense. Remember that a good second serve is considered to be good if it has good pace, good placement, good depth or spin. If the serve has all of these qualities, then their second serve will be not thought of as good second serve but a great one.

Most players stand in the same spot when they are serving. This will allow your opponent to get a good feel of where you are serving and what type of serve you are going to hit. In the deuce court try to slice your serve in order to run your opponent into the alley, along with the serving slice serve, flat or topspin balls into their body and down the middle. If you are able to do this while standing close to the center tee, and while you are standing half way between the singles sideline and the center tee you should have your opponent at a big disadvantage.

In the add court try to hit flat or topspin serves to run your opponent in the alley, along with serving slice flat or topspin balls into their body and down the middle. It will put your opponent at a huge disadvantage if you can serve standing close to the center tee and also from halfway between the singles sideline and the center tee and from the singles sideline as well.

One of the difficult things for a player to achieve is to serve slice, flat, and topspin ball with the same toss. This is very important against top level players. If you can keep your opponent guessing, the quality of their return will not be as high.

Chapter Six

The Receivers' Mental Guide against Strong Serve

If you are playing a right handed player with a strong first serve you have to stay mentally tough, because they are going to get some free points. Your job is to minimize the free points as best as you can. Here's how: Take away the wide serve. This will allow you to get a good feels for how good their serve is down the middle. Start this tactic the first time they serve. Be obvious, and let them know you are taking away the wide serve. Stand half way in the alley. Keep this tactic up for a whole game.

The second game do the opposite. Take away the middle serve for the whole game. Unless it's obvious that you opponents serve down the middle is much better than their wide serve, do not let them get you in the alley. If you stretch for a ball that's been hit down the middle at least you are in the middle of the court after the return. On the other hand if he gets you in the

alley, you are totally off the court. Keep in mind a strong serve does not have to be a player that hits the ball very hard, placement is the key. If your opponent has a strong second serve, the percentages are usually very high they are either serving either topspin to the backhand side or into the body. Usually they will not try a second serve slice wide.

When you are playing a lefty, be confident in knowing that the serve that they are confident in is the slice serve down the middle in the deuce court, and the slice serve to the backhand side in the ad court.

Let your opponent know that you are going to take away their slice serve. Stand at least half way between the singles sideline and the middle of the court in the deuce court, and halfway in the alley on the ad court. Even though they might get some free points by serving to your forehand, odds of that changing soon are very good because you have taken away the serve that they are most confident in.

If your opponent is consistently hurting you on your forehand side, take away the forehand and make them beat you with their best serve. Play the first set all the way out before you make your final decision to change your strategy. When a left handed player is serving a second ball, make them serve to you forehand. If they serve to your backhand do not allow their slice to bounce and move away from you. Attack the ball with your feet.

Chapter Seven

Unnecessary Confusion

Many times when players are on the baseline they are not sure when they should be coming to the net. The confusion is usually caused by the terms short balls and approach shots. Many teachers and players feel that the term short ball is self explanatory. Is a short ball a ball that is hit around the service line, well inside, or a few feet behind the service line? No. A short ball is also the ability to know when you are going to hurt your opponent. This mean you should be moving towards the net, because the ball you hit to hurt your opponent is really an approach shot. The term short ball and approach shot should have the same meaning, but the word "short" brings about the confusion. Players should be aware that balls that are hit in certain areas by their opponent can be approach shots as well. One of the key ingredients of hitting an approach shot is your offensive state of mind before you hit the ball. If you keep these things in mind, your confusion about when to approach the net should subside.

Here are five things that will help you know when you should approach the net:

1. When you serve a first or second serve.
2. When your opponent hits a ball that lands around the service line, or a few feet behind it.
3. When you hit a lob over your opponents head.
4. Whenever you have both feet inside the baseline and you are able to make a good step into the ball.
5. When you know before you hit the ball that your next shot is going to give your opponent trouble.

Most players are more confident when they are on the baseline because they can make a few mistakes and still remain in the point. Whereas, if they approach the net they know that one mistake can mean they will lose the point immediately. As a result, most players approach the net when they have an obvious short ball. Sure, when a player approaches the net, their approach shot has to be much better than if they hit a ball and remain on the baseline. Their reaction time and anticipation has to be faster at the net than on the baseline. When you approach the net there is no room for error in your footwork or the ability to bend your knees properly, particularly against better players. Most players know that there are a few situations in which they should be approaching the net, other than obvious short balls, but their unconscious mind hinders them from doing so. Their unconscious mind knows that they are lacking in their ready position, their volley technique, their footwork, their ability to bend their knees properly or their ability to anticipate and react to the ball quick enough. Again if you are not approaching the net when you should, or you are confused or unsure about when you should be approaching the net, your unconscious mind is protecting one or more weaknesses in your net game. The majority of players spend a lot more time perfecting their baseline game rather than their net game. But in reality they should strive to perfect their net game so that it is at least equal to their baseline game. If a player can get to the point when they are just as confident in their net game as they are in their baseline game, they will view approaching the net as a luxury.

When a player is comfortable approaching the net, they are more aware of the effect their ground stroke have on their opponent. A good example would be if your opponent is on the run after you hit a topspin forehand to their forehand, or if you hit behind them on the forehand side and they have to slice their forehand, you should know that they are on defense. Or if a player has a two-handed backhand and you make them hit a one-handed slice, you should know that they are on defense. If you are playing a player with a one handed backhand and you make them turn their back towards the net, you should know that they are on defense.

If you are watching the ball properly, not only should you see where the ball hits your strings, but you should also see where it hits on your opponents strings. As your ability to do this develops your confidence level should rise, especially when you are approaching the net. Remember, when you approach the net your reaction time and anticipation has to be much faster that if you are on the baseline.

Chapter Eight

Keep on coming

A counter puncher with good topspin strokes and fast feet is a very difficult opponent to defeat. You must maintain a positive and an aggressive state of mind.

Most counter punchers would rather hit on the run and usually their topspin lob is very dangerous when they use it. They are quick and see balls coming off their opponent's strings immediately.

Make sure your approach shots are firm and deep enough to back them up. Be aware when your hit approach shots to their forehands because like most players with a good topspin forehand they can be very late getting to the ball, or hit the ball when its well behind them and still be able to flick the ball by you or over your head with ease. So therefore most approach shots should be hit firm and deep into your opponent's body or firm and deep to their backhand side.

If you decide to hit an approach shot cross-court and you are not thinking about hitting it deep, make sure you either hit an outright winner or you know for sure that your opponent will be in trouble, otherwise you will probably lose the point because you opponent with be able to run over and hit the ball down the line before you can get over there and cover it.

Counter punchers with a good topspin ground strokes usually depend on their ability to get to balls ahead of time which allows them to whip balls by your or get balls by your or get balls to dip at your feet when your feet when you are at the net. Also, when they are in a ground stroke rally, they can get you into the alley when the balls are hit in certain areas of the court with ease. They also depend on their high bouncing topspin balls to keep you on the defense when you are on the baseline. Five key things that should help you when playing against a counter puncher with good topspin groundstrokes:

1. You must be confident in knowing that they usually hit cross-court much better than down the line.
2. Usually their volleys are the weakest part of their game.
3. Do not allow their topspin ground strokes to back you up well behind the baseline. Take the ball on the rise or at your shoulders.
4. Usually they have a big windup, which should mean that balls hit firm and deep should put them in a defensive position.
5. Hitting balls into their body usually turns out to be a very successful tactic.

You cannot allow a good counter puncher to lure you into playing their game. You must keep a positive and aggressive state of mind by continuing to approach the net without hesitation as soon as the opportunity presents itself. Even if you are constantly getting passed after you have hit good approach shots, it is important to keep coming in as often as possible. You cannot second guess yourself, if you do, you should not, be approaching the net. You have to search out the reason or reasons why you are getting passed. Keep in mind that if you don't keep coming you will not find the answers to the problem.

Most counter punchers are at their best when they have a specific target. So you may need to add variety to your approach shots. It is very important for you to know that most players make their best passing shots when they are moving from side to side. So when you are about to hit an approach shot consider hitting a slice that skids and stays low. The low skidding ball should make them come across the baseline a few feet. This will make them hit up. You should be able to vary your slice, making some balls skid into their body, and making some balls skid away. Above all you want this ball around their ankles when they attempt the passing shot.

Most players move to the net after they hit a forehand or backhand down the line. This is understandable because if you cover the half of the court that you hit your approach shot in your opponent should have to hit an excellent passing shot to beat you. You should also know that your opponent's ball can get to you faster if they attempt to pass you down the line. Where as if they hit a good passing shot cross court you have more time to track the ball down. So if you hit cross court you are putting yourself in a vulnerable position because your opponent can pass you cross court or down the line.

The racket technology today allows players to hit incredible shots especially off their forehand side, even if their footwork, racquet preparation, and knee bending is not what it should be. Today's players are also much faster and stronger, which means you could hit your best approach shot to their forehand and get passed easily.

If you are approaching the net you will find that the majority of the time you will be more successful if you hit your approach shot to your opponent's backhand. Most players' success rate is low when hitting passing shots off their back foot, not bending their knees properly, and their racquet preparation is late on the backhand side. So remember that if you hit an approach shot to their forehand their options increase.

Chapter Nine

The Pros and Cons of a Good Topspin Forehand

    Most players with strong topspin forehands are uncomfortable hitting down the line when balls are sliced low to their forehand. Sure they can whip balls cross court easily but the footwork that is needed for hitting down the line usually causes their topspin forehand problems. It is also common for the wrist to get in front of the racquet head, which usually causes chaos when a player attempts a topspin forehand down the line.

    If your opponent has a good topspin forehand, most likely they have a big wind up also. If you are able to hit a ball into the forehand side of their body, approximately a foot or so inside the baseline with as much power as you can generate, you should create a timing problem for them. This timing problem is caused by your opponent's big wind-up prior to hitting their shot. Their big wind up can also lead them to having unbalanced footwork.

Most players with good topspin forehands have problems shortening their strokes. A good example is the return of serve. If you serve a ball wide or into their body with maximum power they most likely will not have time to wind up. They will have to slice the ball or either block it back.

Baseline players with good topspin forehands are always ready for the deep ball, which means for the most part they will not be coming to the net, they will stay a foot or so behind the baseline. So they are not looking to come in unless it's an obvious approach shot. You should hit a firm topspin ball, or under spin, in-between the baseline and the service line, and the next ball hit a foot inside the baseline firm and into the body, and this should upset their timing on their footwork. By not coming in to the net on the first ball, they will be hitting off their back foot on the second ball, along with having to make the necessary adjustments on their wind-up immediately.

Players with good topspin forehands are usually deadly when they are hitting on the run. Their wind up gives them added time to see what type of ball their opponent is looking for. Of course they can whip balls cross court easily, but they can also hit balls down the line with less difficulty when they are on the run.

When your follow through is completed on your forehand your left shoulder should be parallel to the net or facing the net, not pointing towards the back fence. Your left arm should be bent at least at the height of your right shoulder when you finish your follow though. When a players left shoulder ends up pointing towards the back fence, they are really being defensive. A lot of players jump and spin half way around when they are hitting the ball with an open stance on their forehand side. What they are really doing is brushing the ball instead of attacking it. Sure they are putting a lot of effort into hitting the ball that way but are they really playing it safe? If you are not careful, the amount of topspin they put on the ball combined with the height the ball has cleared the net, will cause an error from you, or cause you to hit a short ball.

It takes more confidence for a player to keep their left shoulder either parallel to the net or facing the net when they are hitting their forehand with an open stance. This is difficult because they have all of their weight going into the ball, which means they will be attacking the ball instead of brushing it or guiding it. If a player is really trying to be aggressive, their left foot should be making a strong step toward the net at the same time they are contacting the ball.

Low, short skidding balls are one of the most difficult balls to handle for players even with the best forehands. So a player with a long circle wind-up that goes above their head then below their waist, along with not bending their knees properly will have difficulty handling the slow skidding ball.

Keep in mind if you hit off your back foot, only when you have to, they you will be confident when a situation does arise that will call for you to hit off your back foot. A good example would be if your opponent has you on the defense, and you know as you are tracking the down their ball, you are also watching your opponent while you are approaching the ball late, and contact it when its behind you, while spinning around in a half circle. Conclusion: You have just gone from defense to offense.

Snapping your hip upon contacting the ball plays a major part in creating maximum power on your topspin forehand. Try to refrain from jumping straight in the air, and from jerking your left arm and shoulder, because it will make your head move, which will cause a decrease in your power.

The majority of players today hit their forehands with an open stance because they are more concerned about getting ready for their opponent's reply to their shot than they are about hitting the best ball possible. This is evident because they are constantly hitting off their back foot. When a player hits off their back foot, they tend to brush the ball more instead of driving it. This increases their room for error, as well as their confidence because their ball will be clearing the net with a high arch on it, which makes it difficult for their opponents to attack them. This ball is especially difficult for their opponents to handle if they can make the ball bounce four feet or so inside the baseline with enough height and topspin that would cause the ball to bounce over their opponents shoulder. There are many players who use this strategy because they know that their opponent would have to take the ball on the rise to put them on defense, and they also know that if their opponent is not careful, the topspin and height that they put on the ball has a good chance of creating an obvious short ball.

If you hit your forehand with an open stance you will find that it will cause your opponent more problems if you run around your backhand and hit it. When a player runs around their backhand to hit their forehand it creates a problem for their opponent because their opponent knows that they can put them on defense by hitting in either direction with ease. Whereas if a player hits their forehand with an open stance without running around their backhand, their opponent knows that it would be much easier for them to hit crosscourt than down the line.

The majority of players with an open stance forehand make more errors when they hit the ball down the line, because it is more difficult for them to have the face of the racquet down the line when their follow through is completed. When you hit an open stance forehand it is natural to roll your wrist up an over the ball. But, if you are hitting down the line, you need to keep your wrist laid back, or keep your wrist in front or parallel with your racquet.

One of the main problems the open stance forehand causes is the lack of most players making a good shoulder turn, along with the opposite arm pointing at the ball immediately. If you are hitting a forehand with an open stance while your shoulders are parallel to the net, your will find that hitting the ball down the line is a risky shot. You will also notice that your opponet is covering more cross-court daring you to hit the ball down the line. Remember, that if you make a good shoulder turn you increase your chances of being able to hit the ball just as well down the line as you can crosscourt. It is important for you to be aware of the job that your left arm and shoulder have if you are hitting the ball with an open stance.

Chapter Ten

Winning strategies

If you and your opponent are neutral in the point and your opponent hits a forehand with a lot of heavy topspin into the corner, that has cleared the net about six feet or so, and it lands two feet or so inside the baseline to your forehand what should you do? If you and your opponent are right handed both of you more than likely are hitting forehands. In this type of situation chances are good that you both will be behind the baseline during the rally. Whether you are on offense or defense, it is better to hit the ball deep down the line. Even though both of you are neutral in the point, some players feel that are on the offensive, and some may feel they are on the defensive. If you feel you are on the offensive and decide to go for a winner, or try to put your opponent at a disadvantage by hitting cross-court, your success will be minute. The time it will take your ball to reach its destination and the ability of your opponent to hit late on the forehand side, would most likely not give your ball enough time to get them into trouble in this situation. Your opponent probably will hit a forehand down the line and get you into trouble, or hit an outright winner to either side.

If you feel you are on the offense in this situation, hit the ball deep down the line, because your ball will reach its destination much faster. Shorten your stroke and hit more of a flat, topspin, or shoulder-high ball. This should make the ball reach its destination even faster. By going down the line, the situation changes, because you have an offensive frame of mind in this situation, and your opponent will be on the defensive. Even if your opponent is not late getting to the ball, at most they will end up neutral in the point.

A common winning strategy for most players that are engaged in a baseline rally is to run their opponent into the alley as soon as possible. This is a very effective strategy because it opens up the court, which gives you the option to either hit the ball into their open court or hit the ball behind them. If you hit the ball around or inside the service line to run your opponent into the alley, this could prove to be more effective than if you run them into the alley by hitting a ball halfway between the baseline and the service line.

The majority of players, when they are on the baseline, are looking for their first opportunity to put you on the defense by running around their backhand to hit an attacking forehand usually to your backhand. If you can drive your backhand down the line, to their forehand, a foot or so inside the baseline and the singles sideline, they should be in serious trouble. Your opponent feels that it is too risky for you to attempt to hit a strong backhand down the line, off their powerful forehand. Advanced and top level players know that the high percentage shot is to hit the ball cross-court, trying to get the ball to deep to their backhand. So whenever your opponent hits a strong backhand to your backhand, a strong inside out forehand to your backhand, or a strong forehand down the line to your backhand, and as a reply, if you are able to hit your backhand strong down the line, then what you have is a winning strategy.

In order for you to have a winning strategy against an opponent who is continually attacking you by approaching the net, you must make it known to them immediately that you would rather hit a topspin lob over their backhand side instead of trying to hit an outright winner past them. Once you have convinced them that the lob is your main counter-shot against their attack, their mental state-even if they are hitting good approach shots or backhand overheads will start becoming unglued. Most players who are trying to approach the net as soon as possible have good technique on their volley. They also have a good feel for the damage their approach shot has done, which makes them more likely to be ready for the logical passing shot that you will attempt. Sure a player who tries to beat you by continuously approaching the net is aware that you may lob, or hit low soft slice, balls, or slow rolling topspin balls, but the odds are higher in the favor of you attempting to power the ball by them for an outright winner. It is very important to remember that if your opponent is approaching the net, they must know that there is a good chance you will attempt a lob over their backhand side. In order to force your opponent to be aware of the lob when they approach the net, you will have to sacrifice by losing some points. That's why it is very important that you start lobbing to achieve this goal immedediatley.

Once your opponent has to expect you will probably lob when they approach the net, you can start applying your own winning strategy. Your opponent has to be seriously aware of the fact that you might lob them; they cannot get close to the net as they would like. Not only have you created for yourself more distance between them and the net, you have also created for yourself some more offensive weapons. You can hit a slow rolling, topspin forehand or backhand, making the ball dip at their feet. You can slice forehands and backhands and make the ball stay low at their feet, or blast a forehand or backhand pass them. You could also hit a topspin lob over their forehand side.

Chapter Eleven

Footwork

    There were times when good footwork was a main key to having good ground strokes. But in this era, the topspin groundstrokes have taken a lot of emphasis away from footwork. Footwork, is of course important, but most players today are more concerned with snapping their hips, wrists, and spinning around in a half circle than stepping with their front foot diagonally towards the ball and the net.

    There are three types of footwork: Before, just before and after. The before footwork is the state your feet are in while you are waiting for the ball and how your feet are reacting to the ball once you see where it is going. The just before footwork is the position your feet are in when you are about to contact the ball, and the after footwork is the reaction your feet will make immediately after you make contact with the ball while you are waiting for the next ball.

    Players with good footwork usually get to the ball way ahead of time, but quite often while they are moving after the ball they are not moving with an aggressive mentality. The whole point to moving to a ball is to move in a way that will allow you to make a good diagonal step with the front foot toward the net and the ball upon contact of the ball.

While you are waiting for the ball to come, you should be on your toes with your feet moving in place, along with being one giant step or so behind the baseline. Once your opponent hits the ball, your feet should immediately turn and side step forward at an angle, or half circle, or turn, and side step backward at an angle or half circle.

Keep in mind that the main reasons for having good before footwork as far as the ground strokes are concerned, it that is should cause your frame of mind when you are on the baseline to be an aggressive one.

Just before you make contact with the ball you should be timing your one-two step. The first step is putting your weight on your back foot. The second step is your front foot stepping diagonally towards the ball and the net.

A lot of players today hit with open stance on forehands on purpose. Doing this prohibits you from making a diagonal step towards the ball with your front foot, but you still have time to one-two step. Even though you may be facing the net, your left foot, if you are right handed, or your right foot, if you are left hander, you should be able to make a good step toward the net around the same time you contact the ball.

After you have completed your follow through, your feet should move three or four steps in the same direction. When coming to the net, you should close as quick as possible, and split step when the ball bounces. Afterwards you should be moving your feet anticipating which way the ball is going.

If you are not coming to the net after you have taken your three of four steps forward in the same direction in which you hit the ball, shuffle back behind the baseline about one giant step or so in a half circle. Another important point to remember is, with all of your running, shuffling, and feet moving in place, it should be done on your toes with short quick steps, not giant flat-footed ones.

The before footwork on the volleys is being on your toes with your feet moving. Once you see which direction the ball is going you should turn sideways and step towards the ball as fast as possible.

The just before footwork is timing your steps so that the last step you make just before you hit the ball should be your front foot stepping diagonally toward the net and the ball. You should be at least one and a half arms length or so away from the net. So after you hit the volley, take two or three short steps forward in the direction that you hit the ball shuffle back if you are not an arm-and-a half length away from the net.

An important point to remember about footwork on the volley is that once you make contact with the ball, you should keep side stepping forward until you have completed your follow through. Keep the ball on your strings as long as possible. If you are facing the net and do not have time to turn sideways, you should be able to stutter step forward even though you are facing the net.

When someone hits you a lob, your feet should immediately shuffle sideways so that your left shoulder, if you're are right-handed and your right shoulder if you are left-handed, is pointing diagonally toward the ball. You should be on your toes and feet moving, make sure the ball is coming towards your forehead. When you make contact with the ball you should be on your way back towards the net, not stumbling backwards. If you are a player that hits overheads by jumping ask yourself why. Are your opponent's lobs really that good, which leaves you with no choice but to jump, or are you jumping for no reason? If you are jumping, please keep this in mind. When you jump your feet will usually move backwards because all of your weight is falling backwards: whereas if you hit the ball when it is coming down diagonally towards your forehead, then you will be able to move forward immediately in the direction where you hit the ball as fast as possible. If your feet react to the lob as soon as the ball comes off your opponent's strings, then you should be able to hit most of your overheads without jumping.

The after foot work on the serve is very important. When you make contact with the ball, and you are coming to the net behind it, your feet should quickly move in the direction where you hit the ball. When the ball bounces make your split-step. After your split step keep your feet moving.

If you are not coming to the net after your serve, you should take two or three steps across the baseline then shuffle back behind the baseline immediately.

If you do serve and volley, and you hit a volley stutter-step in the direction that will allow you to cover the half of the court that you hit the volley in. If you are an arm's length away from the net upon completing your volley and movement through the ball, half circle until you are halfway between the service line and the net.

Remember that your opponent is responsible, most of the time, for letting you know when to split step. So even though you may be trying to get to a particular area of the court, it will usually depend on how early or late your opponent is swinging at the ball. This will determine if you will be able to make it to the area you want to be in or if you will you have to make your split-step before you want to.

While you are waiting to return serve, you should be on your toes with you feet moving in place. As your opponent is about to toss the ball, start stutter-stepping forward. Just before they hit the ball split-step. As you make your split-you should be on your toes leaning forward. Once you see the ball, your feet should immediately turn sideways and you should side-step to the ball. Your front foot should be able to make a good diagonal step towards the ball and the net around the same time you are making contact with the ball.

Chapter Twelve

Serving and Volleying

Serving and volleying consistently on both serves and on most surfaces is one of the most difficult styles to maintain in a positive way against an opponent with an excellent return of serve and passing shots.

When you are on the baseline you can win numerous points, games, and matches not bending your knees as much as you should, and with poor racquet preparation. But this is not so when you are serving and volleying. Of course when you are serving and volleying, how well you mix up the speed, spins, and direction of your serve plays a major part in how many points, games, and matches you will win. But moving around on your toes with your back straight, and knees bent as low as possible plays a major role as well.

It is much easier for players to play from the baseline, because when a player is at the net, or coming to the net they must have a certain mentality. Because if they are not bending their knees as much as they should and their footwork is not good, they will lose the point immediately. This is not the case when you are on the baseline.

Most players who are known today for being good serve and volleyers, if they miss their first serve they will stay back on their second serve unless they are playing on grass or on another obvious fast service.

If you are a server and volleyer then that should mean you are serving and volleying consistently on both of your serves. So if you are playing an opponent that is hurting you with their return on your first or second serve, make sure you are mixing up the pace, spin, and direction on your serve. Also make sure you are coming in with your head level with the net, on your toes, with your back straight, and knees low as possible.

Serving and volleying consistently is a lot more physically and mentally tiring than staying on the baseline. If your shot selection is not good when you are at the net or coming to the net you will quickly lose the point. This is not necessarily so if you are on the baseline, because you have more time to regroup if something goes wrong.

If you are serving and volleying you should know the area you should be covering after you serve the ball. If you serve the ball down the middle in the deuce court, usually the return will be somewhere on your backhand side if you are right-handed or you forehand side if you are left-handed. Sure your opponents may win a few points by hitting inside-out backhands, forehands, or slice backhands to your forehand side. But if you generate medium power along with fair depth on your serve, then you shouldn't have to worry about your opponent consistently hitting inside-out backhand, forehands, or slice backhands to your forehand side.

When you are serving wide in the deuce court, ninety-percent of the time your opponent will return the serve to your backhand if you are right-handed. Now if your opponent is left-handed, they can slice their backhand cross-court with less difficulty than going down the line. If they are hitting flat or topspin, usually their return will be on your backhand side.

If you are serving down the middle in the ad-court usually their return will be somewhere on your forehand side if you are right handed. If you serve to the backhand side of a player that hits with two hands, most of their returns with be down the middle or on your backhand side.

The first volley or half volley you hit usually plays a major part in your winning or losing a point. If your opponent is returning serve well, you must know to get your head down to the level of the net with knees bent, along with being on your toes with your back straight. The first four steps you make after you hit your serve should be fast as possible. Go into your split-step when your ball bounces. Once you see where the ball is going, know how hard or low the ball is hit and side step to the ball. Do not let the ball come to you. The only part of your body that should clear the net when you contact the ball is your arm when it straightens out over the net in the direction where you want the ball to go.

The best place to hit the first volley is usually determined by the height the ball is returned over the net and the position your opponent is in after they return your serve. If your opponent hits a return back at your feet, it doesn't matter where you return the ball, but it does matter if it is firm and deep as possible. Whereas if the first volley you hit is at net level or above then you should be able to angle the ball off the court or hit it firm and deep.

Serving is the only time in the game of tennis you get to hit a ball before it is hit to you. So everyone should have an above average serve. Even if you are lacking power you should be accurate. If you have an above average serve, and you are not coming to the net behind it, you are letting your opponent off the hook. Because, even if the return of serve is the best part of your opponents game, and volleying is the worst part of your game, you still will be better off coming in, your opponent will be under more pressure if you come in behind your serve, which should result in their missing a lot of returns and you getting a lot of routine volleys.

Chapter Thirteen

Strokes and Footwork Technique

Topspin Forehand

As soon as the ball comes off your opponents strings, your left hand should point at the ball: at the same time your racquet head should be getting under the ball. Your elbow should be tucked in close to your right side with your racquet head a little above your wrist. Your left are should be diagonally pointing at the ball so that your left foot will be able to make a good diagonal step toward the net and the ball upon contact of the ball. Your behind should be under the ball. You should keep your head still, your back straight while bending your knees. Keep both shoulders up. When you move your left hand upon contact of the ball, keep the left arm in front of you, and it should be somewhat be on the path you want the ball to be on. Keep your wrist firm.

The face of your racquet head should be pointing somewhat toward the ground with your racquet head well below the ball. Once the ball is on your strings you should carry the ball over the net. Your arm should be moving as if you were making a half circle. When you finish your follow through, your racquet should be over the net in the area where you want the ball to go with the face of your racquet pointing somewhat toward the ground.

The power comes from the snapping of your hips upon contact of the ball. Even though your arm may be moving much faster because you are hitting harder, make sure it's all half circle movement. Also once the ball is on your strings, your legs should lift, not straight up, but diagonally. Your left hand should keep you balanced and smooth even if you are in trouble.

A lot of errors occur because of improper footwork, during or after your follow through, along with improper footwork when the ball comes off your opponents strings. As soon as the ball comes off your opponents racquet, and at the same time you should be side-stepping either forward or backward. Do not wait until the ball is on your side of the net before you start getting ready. If your left foot is not stepping toward the ball and the net upon contact with the ball, assume improper footwork.

One hand topspin backhand:

It is very important to get your racquet all the way ready immediately and keep it still until you get ready to step into the ball with your right foot. When you take your racquet back, your racquet head should be well under the ball, and a little bit above your wrist. Whatever level the ball is on, your behind should be under the ball. Keep your head still and your back straight, bend your knees, and keep your wrist firm at all times. Also keep your elbow tucked in close as possible to your right side.

The face of your racquet should be pointing somewhat toward the ground, with your racquet head below the ball. Once the ball is on your strings, you should carry the ball over the net. Your right arm should be moving as if you were making a half circle. When you finish your follow through, your racquet should be pointing in the area where you want the ball to go, with the face of it pointing towards the ground. Your left should be in a straight line with your right arm after your follow through.

The power comes from your legs and the snapping of your hips as your right foot is stepping diagonally towards the ball and the net. Even though your arm will be moving much faster when you want more power, make sure it's a half circle movement. Once the ball is on your strings, your legs should lift powerfully, not straight up but diagonally. When your follow through is completed your knees should still be bent. Also make sure your right foot steps diagonally towards the net and the ball. Remember: The spreading of your left arm upon contact with the ball is very important. It keeps your stroke smooth and accurate even if you are in trouble. Also a lot of balls are missed because of improper footwork before during, and after your follow through. As soon as the ball comes off your opponent's strings, you should immediately get your racquet ready and start moving your feet forward or backward. Do not wait until the ball is on your side of the net before you start getting ready. If your right foot is not able to make a good step toward the net and the ball, in most cases assume that your footwork is not right.

Flat and inside-out-Forehand

If you are in a base line ralley, the flat forehand works best if you are hitting down the line. As you get your racquet ready the face of the racquet should be right behind the ball. The racquet should be a little bit above your wrist. Keep your elbow tucked into your side as much as possible.

Your left foot should step diagonally toward the net and the ball upon contact of the ball. When your left foot makes a step, make sure the ball is in front of your left hand and left foot. Your left arm, and hand, and shoulder should be pointing a little bit over the net where you want the ball to go. When you finish your follow through the face of your racquet should be pointing a little bit over the net where you want the ball to go. If you a hitting a flat forehand, you do not have the luxury of hitting the ball without being down as much as you should. It is very important that your head is at least the level of the ball with your back straight and your behind under the ball.

The inside out forehand is really a flat forehand, unless you do not get around in time, then you will have to pull the ball across your body. If you hit a flat forehand down the line, it's the same thing as running around your backhand and hitting a flat forehand a cross court. So the inside out forehand is an awkward stroke if your footwork is good. If you are able to run around your backhand and step diagonally toward the ball and the net with you left foot, then there is no logical reason for hitting inside-out.

Flat backhand

It is very important that you get your racquet ready immediately after the ball comes off your opponent's strings. Your racquet head should be a little bit above your wrist with the face of your racquet right behind the ball. Whatever level the ball is on your eyes should be on the same level. Keep your back straight. Bend with your knees. Also keep your elbow tucked into your right side as much as possible.

The flat backhand works best if you are hitting the ball down the line. When you finish your follow through, the face of your racquet head should be pointing a little bit over the net towards the spot where you want the ball to go. If you have a one-handed backhand, your left arm should spread in a straight line, as your right foot is stepping diagonally toward the net and the ball upon contact. If you have a two-handed backhand everything is the same. Just let your left hand direct the ball. Do not let your right hand pull against your left.

Forehand Volley

At least ninety per-cent of the time, if a player is an excellent volleyer, their forehand volley will not be as good as their backhand volley.

It is very important on the forehand volley that you have enough angle on your racquet head. The face of your racquet should be pointing diagonally towards the sky. This will allow you to get more under-spin. Your racquet head should be above your wrist. Your wrist should be firm at all times. Your elbow tucked in close; eyes should be ball level, back straight and bend with your knees.

As soon as the ball comes off your opponents strings, you should turn your shoulders diagonally towards the ball and side step. Make sure your left foot step towards the ball. You should be trying to make contact with the ball before it starts to drop.

Many players and coaches believe that punching the ball on the volley is the most effective way of volleying. Sure if the ball is above the net it doesn't matter if you punch it or follow all of the way through it. If the ball is at the level of the net or any where below it, you should slice all the way through until your arm straightens out and is pointing over the net toward the spot where you want the ball to go.

Your left hand should let you know exactly when you should hit the ball. Your left hand should be pointing diagonally at the ball. When you move it upon contact with the ball, it should be over the net.

Backhand Volley

It is very important that your wrist is firm, and your racquet head is a little above it. Your racquet should remain in front of your body at all times. Even when your shoulders turn, your racquet should stay in front of your body. A lot of players take their racquet behind their body or on the side of their body for more power. But the power comes from stepping diagonally toward the ball and the net upon contact of the ball when you are following all the way through the ball as firm as you can. Do not take your racquet back and swing for more power. So if your racquet stays in front of you at all times, that means that the ball will be in front of you at all times. When your right foot makes the step towards the ball and the net, the ball should be in front of your right foot when you contact it.

Your left arm is very important for balance and direction. Just as your right foot is stepping toward the net and the ball, your left arm should spread in a straight line. Once the ball is on your strings your right arm should spread in a straight line, with your racket pointed over the net where you want the ball to go. Your left arm should straighten out completely in the opposite direction of your right arm. Both arms should be in one straight line pointing over the net at the spot where you want the ball to go. You should be holding your racquet as if you are shaking hands with someone. This means you should have no trouble getting underpin.

Backhand and Forehand Half Volley

You must have your knees down and you back straight for your half volley to be effective.

As you are preparing to hit a half volley, your racquet should be in front of your body as though you were going to hit a volley. it is very important that your follow through is firm, and your racquet should be pointing over the net a little bit toward the spot where you want the ball to go.

It is very important that your feet move through the ball toward the spot where you want the ball to go. If your feet are not able to move the forward as you are following though the ball, at least the first move your body should make is forward.

Your head should be at the level of the net. The only thing that should be above the net after your follow through is completed is your racquet.

If you are hitting a backhand half volley, your left knee should almost touch the ground. Keep in mind that this should be done while you are keeping your back straight as possible. Keep your shoulders up. Hit the ball in front of your left hand on your forehand and your right foot on your backhand. Also, spread your left arm upon contact with the ball on your backhand. You should spread your left arm the same way as you would on the one handed backhand ground stroke and the volley.

Overheads

The preparation of your racquet and your left arm and shoulder is very important when you are hitting overheads. As soon as the ball comes off your opponents strings your racquet should immediately get all the way ready. That means the last place your racquet is at before you hit the ball should be the first place it should be when the ball comes off your opponents strings. Your left arm should be straighten out completely, while pointing diagonally toward the ball. This should be done instantly. If you let the ball drop, it should hit you in the forehead. Your left shoulder should immediately point diagonally towards the backhand alley. Keep your back straight at all times.

Once your left arm points at the ball, it's up to your feet to keep the ball coming down towards your forehead. You should be side stepping around with your left shoulder sideways. When you make contact with the ball, and find yourself not being able to come back towards the net in the area where you hit the ball, assume your footwork is not right. It is important that you are on your way to the net as you are completing your follow though. You must make contact before it reaches you left hand. When you drop your left arm just before you contact the ball, drop it somewhere above your waist, not down by your side. Keep both shoulders up. When you have completed your follow through, your racquet and left arm should be above your waist.

Your left shoulder should remain sideways until after your follow through is completed. Once your left shoulder points diagonally towards the backhand side, this will allow you to disguise your overhead. You can either hit flat to the backhand side or slice it to your opponent's forehand side. If the lob is anywhere around the service line or inside of it, you should be able to angle the ball off the court. If your opponent hits a deeper lob, give yourself room for error, aim for the service line on their backhand side.

It is very important to remember to keep your head up after you drop your left arm just before contact with the ball. You should see the ball when it hits your strings, if you look over the net after you see the ball hit your strings, look without turning your head.

It is also crucial that you stay on your toes with your feet moving with short quick stepping movements, even if the ball is coming down right to you. Do not wait for the ball flat footed. It is important to have rhythm with your feet. Actually, your feet should only stop moving for a split second and that's just before you make contact with the ball.

Topspin Forehand and Backhand Lobs

When you are hitting a topspin lob, it is very important to hit the ball over your opponent's backhand side. For your lob to be effective, it should be hit when your opponent knows you have at least one other shot that you can hit easily. On the forehand topspin lob it is important that your left arm stays above the net. Your racquet head should be well below the ball. Contact the ball in front of your left hand and left foot. Once the ball is on your strings you should hit up diagonally on a straight line. Do not start hitting over the ball until you have almost completed your follow through. This should assure that you have enough height and depth on your lob.

If you know that the lob you are going to hit will be over the backhand side of your opponent, you should be taking a few steps forward after your follow through. Your weight should be on your front foot, which means you should be able to hit the lob while your weight is going forward not backward.

When your racquet head is under the ball on the forehand lob, the face of your racquet head should be pointing towards the ground. When you finish your follow through, the face of your racquet should be over the net and pointed all the way towards the ground. If you are a right handed player, playing against another right handed player, in most cases, you should be hitting the forehand lob down the line.

When you are hitting a backhand topspin lob, you should be hitting it cross-court on your opponent's backhand side, keeping in mind that it takes longer for the ball to get over your opponent's head. When you hit your topspin backhand lob, the ball should be hit more flat with little topspin. Do not follow all the way through the ball; stop your follow through about halfway. It's almost like you are punching a volley, but the difference is that you do follow though very briefly. Since the ball is more or less ricocheting off of your strings you must be confident to know that you don't have to hit the ball hard at all. The angle you hitting on, along with contacting the ball mainly flat, will cause the ball to go over your opponents head before he or she can react.

Keep your back straight, behind under the ball, and bend with the knees. You must hit the ball before it passes your right foot. When you step into the ball your left hand should spread but not all the way, about half way on the one handed backhand lob.

At least ninety-percent of the time when you are hitting a topspin lob, you should be on the offense. However if you find yourself on the defense, you should be trying to hit the lob as high as possible on a slight angle. Defensive lobs usually hit flat, so that means you finish your follow through with the face of your racquet pointing towards the sky at a slight angle. Usually if you hit a defensive lob, you will be on your back foot. Keep your shoulders up with your back straight and head still. Your racket should be ready quickly. Upon contact with the ball, your arm and whole body should be firm as possible, not wobbling. Remember, hitting the ball as high as possible on a slight angle is the main key point in hitting a defensive lob.

Chapter Fourteen

Serve Techniques

First Serve

Keep your back straight and your shoulders up until your follow though is complete. When you toss the ball up, your left arm should straighten out completely. You should release the ball diagonally out in front of your body and a little bit to the right. If your arm is bent at the point when you make contact with the ball, then either your toss was not high enough, your back did not remain straight, your shoulders did not stay up, you hit the ball on the way up, or you let the ball drop. Once you toss the ball up you want to hit it when it stops at the top of your toss, which is call the apex, or still point, before it starts to drop, not on its way down.

The main source of power and accuracy is in the ability to keep your left shoulder up and sideways as long as possible until your follow though is completed. When you drop your left arm after tossing the ball, you should drop it somewhere around or above your waist, not by your side. When you finish your follow through your racquet should be somewhere around your waist if not higher.

Your racquet should not be lower than the net. It is equally as important to keep both shoulders up, and keep your head up until after your follow though has been completed. If you have to see where the ball is going to get a feel for your opponents return, look out of the side of your eyes, not by turning your head.

Another important aspect of the serve is the rhythm of your feet, if you are not serving and volleying. If you are serving and volleying your feet should automatically move forward through the ball which allows all of your weight to be transferred into the ball. This is called kinetic energy, the energy of motion. But many times when a player is staying back on their serve, they do not take enough steps forward in the direction they want the ball to go. As you are completing your follow through, your feet should take at least three to four steps over the baseline in the direction you want the ball to go. It is important to get all of your weight naturally behind your serve, rather than to be ready for the return and not have half of your natural weight behind the ball. If you are three to four steps over the baseline after your serve is completed, shuffle back behind the baseline as fast as you can after your serve.

If your opponent hits a return of serve for a winner, or one that gets you into trouble, do not give up on your strategy. You should know immediately after the point where the break-down was, whether it was your serve or your footwork.

When taking the racquet up to hit the ball, bend your arm as if you are making a muscle with your arm. The area that you contact the ball on your strings, as well as the type of motion your arm makes after the ball hits your strings, determines the amount of speed and type of spin that will be on the ball. If you are going for an ace in the deuce court, or trying to get your opponent into the alley you should keep your left shoulder sideways and contact the ball in the top right hand corner of your racquet. If you are going for an ace down the middle, you should contact the ball around the middle of your strings. If you decide to hit a kick serve, you should contact the ball around the middle of your strings as well.

On the kick serve, you should toss the ball straight above your head. Time the toss so that when your body is moving across the baseline the ball will be straight above your head when you make contact. The motion of your arm should be as if you are making a half circle.

The motion of your arm on the flat serve is the face of your racquet straight through the ball. So that means your arm should move in a straight line at your target.

The motion of your arm on the slice serve is at the point of impact. Your wrist will automatically break and your arm will move to the right for a split second.

One of the main keys when you are serving a slice, flat, or topspin ball is knowing where you are contacting the ball and how your arm should be moving once you know what type of serve you are going to hit.

Second Serve

It is very important on the second serve for you to toss the ball straight above your head. This should be done if you are serving topspin or kick serve, not flat or slice. When you release the ball on a kick serve, your knees should be bent and waiting for the ball to stop at the top of the apex. Once the ball stops, your legs should spring up after the ball. Your back should remain straight from start to finish. When you drop your left arm after tossing the ball, it should drop somewhere in front of your body above your waist, not by your side.

When you finish your follow through, your racquet should be somewhere above your waist. If you are hitting topspin or a kick serve to your opponent's backhand, your arm should be moving as if you are making a half circle. Your grip should be as if you were hitting a one-handed topspin backhand. (Backhand grip)

This should make it a lot easier to get maximum topspin on the ball with little effort. You should contact the ball around the middle of your strings. You should hit up and then over the ball. Hitting up means the ball should clear the net and the hitting over the ball means the topspin will bring the ball down into the court before it flies out.

If you are hitting a second serve to your opponent's forehand, you should hit the ball using the top inside corner of your racquet. If you toss the ball straight above your head, your opponent will naturally think you are going to serve to their backhand. With this method you will catch your opponent off guard. This will cause confusion in your opponents mind regarding your second serve. You can toss the ball out in front and a little bit to your right and slice the ball to your opponent's forehand. If you contact the ball in the top inside corner of your strings, the ball will hit and break away from your opponent. You will probably serve an ace or an un-returnable ball. The problem with this method is you don't have any room for error and a good player will know by your toss that you are not serving a kick serve to their backhand.

Even if you are staying back on your second serve when you finish your follow through, you should at least be two or three steps inside the baseline. When your legs spring up after the ball your left shoulder should be diagonally going up and forward. When you start to hit over the ball, your feet should be in the air over the baseline.

Chapter Fifteen

Balance and Placement

If you are a right handed player, your left hand, arm, and shoulder are key factors in how good your balance is going to be. (If you are left handed, I'm talking about your right arm, hand and shoulder.)

Also your left arm, hand and shoulder play a major role in keeping the ball on the plain in which you want it to be on. Six things to remember for good balance and placement.

1. Keep both shoulders up
2. Keep your back straight and bend with your knees.
3. Keep your left hand, arm, and shoulders on the same plain you want the ball to be on if you are right handed.
4. Your racquet should be pointing over the net at the spot where you want the ball to go until the ball is completely off your strings.
5. After you hit a volley or overhead take two steps in the direction you want the ball to go and to shuffle

back if you are not an arm's length and a half away from the net. On the overhead and volleys cover the half of the court where you hit the ball.
6. If you are hitting a ground stroke and not coming to the net behind it, take three to four steps forward after you hit the ball. If you are in front of the baseline shuffle back behind it. Stay least one giant step behind the baseline. A important point, to remember is when you hit the ball take a few steps in the direction in which you want the ball to go.

Two handed topspin backhand:

It is very important that you keep your elbow tucked in close to your body on the two-handed backhand, as soon as the ball comes off your opponents strings, get your racquet head under the ball immediately. This should be done with your elbow in. Whatever level the ball is on, your behind should be under it. Your racket head should be a little bit above your wrists. Keep both wrist firm as possible at all times. Your back should be straight. If you have to bend, let it be with your knees only.

If you really think about what hand is responsible for the spin and direction of the ball on the two-handed topspin backhand, you will find that it's your left hand. Do not allow your right hand to pull against your left. Let your left hand be moving as if you were making a half circle. When you finish your follow-through the face of your racquet should be pointing somewhat toward the ground. Your racquet should be pointing over the net in the direction where you want the ball to go.

The power comes from your hip snapping upon contact with the ball as you right foot making a good diagonal step toward the net and the ball. Upon contact make sure the ball is in front of your right foot and toward the net. You left hand will be moving fast if you are trying to generate maximum power, but make sure it's a half circle movement. Most balls are missed due to improper footwork. As soon as the ball comes off your opponent strings you should immediately get your racquet ready and start moving forward or backward. Do not wait until the ball is on your side of the net before you start getting ready. If your right foot is not able to make a good diagonal step toward the net and the ball, upon contact, then in most cases you can assume your footwork is not right. Take a least two steps in the direction you want the ball to go as you are completing your follow-through.

One handed slice backhand

It is important to get your racquet ready as soon as the ball comes off your opponent's strings. When your racquet is ready, make sure it is all the y way ready. This means that the next move that your racquet makes once you get it ready is forward, not taking it back again then forward. When you take your racquet back it should be right behind the ball with your wrist firm and your racquet a little bit above your wrist. Keep the elbow tucked in close to your body. This should be done when you first start getting your racquet ready. Your back should be straight as possible. You should bend with your knees. You should have your eyes on the same level as the ball.

The face of your racquet should be pointing diagonally towards the sky. You should contact the ball at the same time as your right foot is stepping diagonally toward the net and the ball. You should slice straight through the ball. As you right foot is making the diagonal step, your arm should be gliding smoothly through the ball. When you finish your follow through your racquet should be pointing over the net where you want the ball to go.

The spreading of your left arm in the direction you want the ball to go is a major factor in how good your accuracy and balance will be. Your left arm should spread in a straight line at the time you make contact with the ball and until your follow through is completed.

Lots of unforced errors occur because of improper footwork, before, during, or after your opponent hits the ball. As soon as the ball comes your opponents strings you should get your racquet ready and start moving forward backward or in a half circle. Do not wait until the ball gets on your side of the net and get ready. If your right foot is not stepping towards the net and the ball assume your footwork is not right. Take at least two steps in the direction you want the ball to go as you are completing your follow though.

Final thoughts:

Remember to stay focused on achieving the ultimate goal in tennis every point you play. If you do this you cannot help but be more confident because your strategy is now automatic. You will also experience a major rise in confidence because you will be focusing on winning the point instead of hoping your opponent will lose it.

Avoid letting your racquet compensate for you not physically applying yourself as you should. The racquet technology today allows players to hit more great shots that ever before with poor footwork, and no knee bending. The racquets today also give the majority of players a secure feeling that they are strong enough in the shoulders, abs, and hips when they really are not.

Keep in mind that there are three categories of footwork. The footwork you have while waiting on the ball. The footwork you have when you are tracking the ball your opponent has hit to you, and the footwork you have after you have returned the ball your opponent has hit to you. Strive as much as possible to stay on your toes with your feet shuffling in place while you are in the ready position, more with the short stutter steps when you are tracking ball, making your last step the longest. Try to avoid hitting off your back foot unless it is necessary. Remember the footwork you have after you hit a ball is just as important as your hitting a good ball. Therefore if you are not approaching the net after you hit the ball, half circle a giant step behind the baseline towards the middle. If you are coming to the net after you hit the ball move quickly to the service line in the half you hit the ball in.

Strong shoulders, abs, and hips are associated with good posture. Pretend that you are trying to force your chest to rip through your shirt. In order for you to do this your back would have to be firm and straight with your shoulder blades locked back. Your abs and hips have to be firm and strong. If you can master hitting all of your strokes while having good posture, your game will accelerate immediately to a higher level.

Once a player is in excellent shape, then how successful they will be is determined by the quality of their mind. Study your tennis personality to see if it brings fear to your opponent. Try to establish a tennis personality that will bring about an uneasy feeling to your opponent every time they look at you whether they are winning or losing.

Look for my next book which will be out soon. I will reveal my secret in an area of your game that is vital if winning is your goal. The area of your game I am referring to is mental toughness.